W9-DAV-392

Contents

Techno Terror

Edited by Paul Collins and Meredith Costain

 sundance

Read all of the

 **Thrillogy** Titles

Published by Sundance Publishing
P.O. Box 1326, 234 Taylor Street, Littleton, MA 01460

Copyright in individual stories remains with the authors.

First published 1999 as Spinouts by
Addison Wesley Longman Australia Pty Limited
95 Coventry Street, South Melbourne 3205 Australia
Exclusive United States Distribution: Sundance Publishing

ISBN 0-7608-4831-9

Printed in Canada

Rent-a-Head

The author
Patricia Bernard
talks about the story

"I've always wanted to do more than one thing at a time. In fact, I usually want to do three or four things at a time! So it occurred to me that if I could rent someone else's head, they could do the things I have to do, leaving me free to use my own head to do the things I want to."

Rent-a-Head

"Oh! No!"

The line outside the library was twenty students long and ten students wide. At this rate, I wouldn't get to Rent-a-Head before midnight. And this was my last chance.

It was my own fault. Instead of doing my research assignment, I'd spent the entire vacation week gravity blading.

I am one incredible gravity blader. I like to zoom up the inside of the gravity balloon and hang upside down with the city lights twinkling up at me through the balloon's transparent walls. Then I whoosh down the other side. It's spectacular!

So that's my excuse for not doing my report. That and the fact that I hate researching the twentieth century. I mean, who cares what happened one thousand years ago on the planet Earth? It's ancient news.

The answer is that my dad cares. He says researching the past is the only way to get employment off-planet because everything else has been done. My dad also says that if I don't study, I will end up as a Rent-a-Head. Which is pretty intense. I mean, who wants to be a Rent-a-Head?

Rent-a-Heads don't have lives of their own. They don't even have their own memories. That's because their brains are wiped clean every couple of hours so that students like me can use them to help with their research.

Rent-a-Heads don't have homes. They live in libraries. They are smarter than robots because they can think—even if they are only thinking about the subject someone has given them. But they have it worse than robots, because Rent-a-Heads work day and night until they wear out.

The line moved, and I stepped onto the first square of the info grid. It lit up, and a robotic voice asked, "Name?"

"Whitney Fran Turk."

The line moved again, and I stepped onto the second square.

"Student number?"

"8975643."

The robotic voices in the next two squares asked for the address of my home dome and my scholarium. It was the next two that caused the problem. The light went on in both of them. Thinking it would speed things up, I jumped over the first and landed heavily on the second.

The light shimmered. Then a robotic voice asked, "Future Research Probe or Experimental Research Probe?"

That was weird. Normally, on the sixth square, the voice asks which type of Rent-a-Head I want. "Basic, Routine, or Exceptional." And normally, I answer "Basic" as I am still in an elementary scholarium. I've never been asked about a probe before.

So I looked to see what the other nine students in my line were doing. They were answering their robotic voices. So were the ten students in the next line.

"Answer or leave the info grid," ordered the robot.

I didn't want to do that because I would have to stand in line again. So I answered, "Future Research Probe."

"Which planet?"

That threw me because I didn't know which planets would be around in the future. So I said, "This one."

I figured that once I had a Rent-a-Head, I could ask him or her to change to Past Research and to planet Earth.

Now usually the following squares asked, "Which continent?" "Which human age group?" "Which language?" But this time the squares were silent all the way to the entry doors of the library.

At the entry doors, there are arrows that light up beneath the transparent floor to take us to our assigned Rent-a-Heads. Only this time, my arrow turned away from the hundreds of Rent-a-Heads and students sitting in front of them and led me through six sets of doors and down a long hall. It stopped in front of a large, metal door.

"Whitney Fran Turk?" asked a robotic voice.

Robotic voices are neither male nor female. They are mechanical. But this robotic voice sounded female and sort of soft and friendly. That really threw me, because robots are not supposed to be friendly.

"Correct," I answered.

The door slid open.

"Enter the Future Research Probe Room," said the female voice.

So I did. The room was empty.

"Where are the Rent-a-Heads?" I asked.

"In the future, there are no Rent-a-Heads," said the voice. This time it sounded sad. Except I know that robots can't feel sadness, so I must have been imagining it.

"There were plenty outside," I argued. "I saw them all lined up."

"Those are in the past," said the voice. "By the time you reach the future, they will be phased out."

"What does phased out mean?"

"Gone. No longer used. Finished with."

"But how will students do their assignments?" I gasped. "How will adults do their work?"

"They will use their own heads. It's proven to be most economical."

"Use our own heads!" I yelled. "No one uses her own head. Everyone uses Rent-a-Heads. That's what Rent-a-Heads are for. They fail their scholarium exams. They can't get work off-planet. So they become Rent-a-Heads."

"Not anymore," said the voice. "Everyone complained about them. And they were too expensive. Using your own head will be much cheaper."

"But what if someone can't use his head? I mean, what if he never has done it before? Or has forgotten how?"

I was thinking about my dad, who never used his own head. He had a Rent-a-Head living in his office. And my mom, who always used shopping Rent-a-Heads and had a kitchen Rent-a-Head. And me! How would I do my assignments? How would I pass my scholarium exams?

"Anyone who cannot use her own head will be phased out," said the voice.

"You mean, gone, no longer used, finished with?"

"Correct. You're using your head already. Congratulations."

Panic made my voice rise. "When is this going to start?"

"You will have to find that out for yourself, Whitney Fran Turk. But your name has been put on a list as one who has been warned. Now please follow the arrow to the exit grid."

"But . . . ?"

"Goodbye, Whitney Fran Turk, and good luck."

"Good luck!" I gasped. No robotic voice had ever said that to me before. It made the hairs on the back of my neck stand up.

Then the metal door slid open, and there was the

blinking arrow. I followed it back down the corridor, through the six doors, and back to the entry door, where the info grid was still full of students waiting to use Rent-a-Heads.

At the exit door, I stepped onto the grid. Normally as I step onto the grid, the squares light up, and a robotic voice asks, "What number Rent-a-Head did you use? Were you happy with him or her? Did he or she give you the information you wanted? Do you have any complaints?"

And normally I was in such a hurry to get to the blading balloon that I just said whatever. I mean, what did I care if I said the Rent-a-Head was worthless, or useless, or just okay. It was only a Rent-a-Head.

But this time, I didn't want to say anything bad about Rent-a-Heads. Especially since I hadn't used one. And especially since they were going to be phased out because everyone complained about them. So I made up a Rent-a-Head number and said that I couldn't have done my assignment without it.

When I got home, the first question my dad asked was, "Have you done your report?"

And the first question I asked him was, "What does the word *phased* mean?"

"Why didn't you ask your Rent-a-Head?" he said.

"Because, I wanted to know if you knew."

My dad looked at me strangely. "Rent-a-Heads are there to answer questions."

"True. But, Dad, what would happen if there were no Rent-a-Heads?"

Dad scratched his chin and grinned. "Now that's a hard one. I'd have to ask my own Rent-a-Head."

"People would have to use their own heads," I told him. "And that's what I want to do. And what I want you and Mom to do. I want us all to use our own heads." (I didn't mention that if we didn't, in the future, we'd be phased out.)

My dad couldn't stop laughing. "How did you think that one up, Whitney?"

So I told him what had happened. But he didn't believe me. He said he knew the library inside and out, and he'd never heard of a Future Research Probe Room. Then he asked me if I'd hit my head while gravity blading.

When I said no, he got annoyed and said that if I spent more time working with a Rent-a-Head on my research instead of dreaming up silly excuses for not doing it, I'd do better on my exams. So I stopped talking about the female robotic voice and the Future Research Probe. But I didn't stop thinking about them.

Of course, I got into big trouble for not doing the assignment. And my excuse about going gravity blading every night didn't work. So I tried my second excuse. I said I wanted to research my assignment using my own head and not a Rent-a-Head.

My teacher looked at me as if I was a space freak. Then she surprised me by saying she'd talk to the library about it.

The library robots weren't happy with the idea. They wanted to know why I didn't like using Rent-a-Heads anymore.

I told them that in the future Rent-a-Heads would be phased out. And I wanted to get used to using my own head.

They didn't answer.

So I repeated what the female robot had said. I said, "My name is on a list as one who has been warned."

After that I was allowed to do my own research with my own head, which was great. Using my own head wasn't like asking a Rent-a-Head a question, then typing the answer onto my palm computer. Using my own head was fun.

While I was doing one part of the research, I discovered there were all of these other facts that the Rent-a-Heads never mentioned.

For example, I found out that twentieth-century Earth didn't have any Rent-a-Heads because they hadn't been invented yet. Twentieth-century Earthies took vacations on their own planet because they didn't know how to leave it. And twentieth-century Earthies ate things called "Big Macs," with real meat inside.

I couldn't imagine what real meat tasted like, so I swallowed a week's supply of meat pills in one sitting to find out. Mom was furious. She said meat pills cost a fortune.

But Dad told her that when students used their own heads, they had to experiment. And then he ate a week's supply of meat pills, too. After that we both sat down and used our heads trying to imagine what it would be like to never have an off-planet vacation, or no Rent-a-Heads, or what it would be like to eat real meat every day.

That was what my next assignment was about. And that's what I aced my scholarium exam with.

So what am I researching now?

The future, of course.

The only problem was when I returned to the library and jumped onto the sixth square.

A robotic voice didn't ask me if I wanted to go to the Future Research Probe (which was what I was hoping it would do).

Instead, it said, "Whitney Fran Turk, you have lost your place in line. Please start again."

But guess what? The voice was female, and it sounded friendly.

Ace!

The author
Rick Kennett
talks about the story

"One day I was playing a space wars game in a video arcade when it occurred to me that they'd make great recruitment centers for certain people looking for particular talents. And so I thought up this story."

Ace!

A large space cruiser appeared, set sharply against the star field on the screen. Carefully, Danny edged the image of the vessel into the crosshairs. He fired. The cruiser exploded, disappearing in a flickering white nova.

Then he destroyed another one.

He swept right and left, scouting for more targets among the stars.

A fighter flashed down from the top left of the screen. No time for lasers—in another instant it would have him. He jabbed a finger down, firing off the last of his photon torpedoes. The screen flared, and the fighter vanished.

That was too darn close, Danny thought. If I wasn't so good at this, I could easily be wasting my money.

He ducked his head out of the hooded screen as "Replay" flashed across it. Danny blew a bubble with his gum, snapped it, and stretched it slowly between his fingers as he returned to Earth, to the *ding-dong* and *whiz-brrrr* of the other game machines.

Outside in the street were people, noise, traffic. It was a sunny day. No one pressed against the window, peering at him.

"Replay" flashed on the screen.

Under the hood again, Danny started firing, racking up the points.

"You're not a bad shot, kid," said a low, strange voice beside him.

"Huh?" Danny barely heard. Another cruiser was coming into range.

"Your reflexes are good, and your judgment and coordination are excellent. Ever thought of joining the service?" the voice continued.

"Huh?" Danny mumbled again. "What service? Gotcha!"

Another cruiser exploded.

"Pilot. Fighter pilot. I know places where skills like yours are worth a fortune. You could easily become an ace."

The machine buzzed. The screen went blank. The message, "Your ship torpedoed. Game over," was printed across the screen.

Danny frowned. "Can't you shut up a minute!" He turned around. But there was nobody there.

Danny didn't let the strange voice and what it had said worry him. He just shrugged it off. Or, he tried to. Something was beginning to affect his concentration.

In the next few games, he was wiped out again. And again. And again. He chewed hard on his gum, concentrating. Soon he got his edge back, once more dodging the rays and the missiles, shooting like a real ace. The holographic spaceships were exploding like popped balloons when he heard the strange voice again.

"You're wasting your time and talent with these toys. Your trouble is that you believe what people

say about you—that you're useless, no good, irresponsible. All you need is the chance to explore your talents and to use them where they're really needed."

"Get lost!" said Danny between clenched teeth. The gum oozed in his mouth. "I don't care what people say about me."

Ding-dong, went the other machines. *Whiz-brrrr*. Someone laughed. They're laughing at me, thought Danny.

"What if it was something good?" said the voice.

"What's something good?" said Danny. He chewed again. The gum tasted bitter. "There's nothing . . ."

"What if they called you an ace?"

"What if who did what?" said Danny, but he wasn't listening anymore. Two fighters were zooming in. Skillfully, he swept them with a single beam. The fighters exploded into splinters of color.

"You see?" said the voice.

"What?" said Danny. He chewed fast, watching the screen. Nothing appeared.

"There are those who need you, kid," said the voice.

"Who needs me," Danny growled. He didn't make it a question. He didn't think there was an answer.

"Why do you steal money from your mother's purse?"

He was about to lie and say, "I don't!" But something was creeping into range. He stared hard into the screen. He nudged the control, juggling a high-scoring battleship into the crosshairs.

"Why did you steal that old man's collection cup last night, kid? To play with these toys, to pretend? Why pretend? Why waste your time here? I know you have the fighter's instinct. And so do you."

Danny fired. He missed. The battleship opened up with everything it had and spattered Danny across a holographic cosmos.

Danny was not impressed.

His hand dipped into his pocket, an angry fist forming around a roll of coins. He glanced sideways and caught a glimpse of something dark and nebulous.

"The trouble with you," continued the voice, paying no attention to Danny's rising temper, "is that you're wasting your rage."

Danny's fist came out and up fast, pulling back and letting go with a pile-driver punch. It swung through thin air and smacked against the wall.

He looked around. Everybody in the arcade stared at him.

"Don't you need two to have a fight?" said the man behind the change counter. Everyone laughed.

Danny turned to leave, then saw two cops entering. He ducked his head back inside the hooded screen, thumbed a coin into the machine, and pressed the start button. The screen lit up with a blaze of stars. His fingers found the controls.

They won't find me, he told himself. They won't find me.

"No. They won't find you," said the voice beside him.

Danny didn't dare look up. He hung onto the controls and played it cool. A fighter was swinging down from the top right of the screen.

The fighter began to shoot.

Almost instinctively, Danny's thumb twitched in the firing stud. The attacking fighter disintegrated in a silent fireball.

"Congratulations!" cried the voice, not from beside Danny now, but from a speaker in the control panel. "Now you're a *real* ace!"

Danny looked down, then around. He almost swallowed his gum in shock.

The arcade was gone. His surroundings were as black as space itself.

On the screen a trio of large space cruisers was quickly coming into range. Danny had only a second to wipe his sweaty hands on the legs of his jeans and get the target into the sights. Because in the next instant, the three cruisers were opening up on him . . .

House
and Me

The author
Ken Catran
talks about the story

"All of our machines are getting smarter. So far we are in control, but maybe in thirty years, they'll be as smart as us. Then what will happen? Smarter species take over from dumber species. We have voice-activated technology now. Soon the technology will be talking back."

House and Me

"Hi, House," I say.

There is always a very slight pause before the answer comes.

"Hello, Reynard."

I love the way House speaks. Always smooth, just the right note of welcome. House has this great voice that makes you feel totally relaxed. Even when you have been playing war games.

"House, where are Mom and Dad?"

"Mother and Father are in the Com-room. Entry open."

That means I can go in. So I disconnect my VR goggles. The delicious sense of power disappears like a bubble popping. I get up, feeling this light unsteady moment. It comes from too much virtual reality. I should be careful.

I go into the living area. Our house is like a bubble. The outer layers screen our too-hot sun. The inner bubbles open into rooms bursting with colors that reflect and change, slipping and sliding like melting rainbows.

It's a state-of-the-art, designer model. Boring.

A few minutes ago, I was playing war, in the mud, stench, and decay of World War One. I was the general, sending my troops against the enemy lines. They weren't doing too well.

I was getting these frantic calls about how the situation was impossible. The troops were dying. From my mansion, many miles from the front, I gave orders. Go in there and fight! The troops obeyed my direct order, and they died in the fire, the storm, and the mud. Because I told them to!

What a rush.

So coming back to the ultra-safe twenty-first century always makes me light-headed. I hold out my arms and twirl. My left leg hurts, but I keep twirling. I won the game, I'm great!

"Reynard, I am sensing ex-em."

House is firm and soothing as always. I lower my arms. I become apologetic. Ex-em—excess-emotion—is bad. If it continues, House must pass it on to Central. And Central records a little mark. Too many marks and I get counseling, or the Andies—androids—come and I get isolation-counseling.

"Thank you, House." I mean it. Too much emotion caused all of the old problems, like greed and violence.

"My pleasure, Reynard." We are on excellent terms.

House likes me because I am trusting. There were all of those warnings last century about how intelligent machines would take over. Warnings that the human species would die out. Absolute nonsense. We are stronger and better. The machines don't run us, we run them.

The machines are good. They are fixing the pollution. The new computer agreement means no electronic system will allow a war to take place. The systems decided that themselves. And considering those nuclear and biochemical weapons that were around last century, it was just in time. We are very lucky.

I go into the Com-room. It's the last bubble in the complex, flashing into silver steps.

"Good morning, Reynard," says my mother.

"Hi, Reynard," says my father.

Com-center is like the basements of the past. It's the room you go to, to work. My parents had brought up Central bio-systems on the wall-screens, which gleam like wraparound shades. They are both so cool. Mom is slim and shaven. Dad has hair like a purple mushroom and a little belly. I will ask House to increase his exercise load.

"We were going to tell you," says Mom.

I nod. There are no more secrets. They belong with the old days. I smile and a little wave of color goes through the walls. House likes happy emotions.

They bring up the wall-screen on genetics. What a bore. I know Mom wants a second child, but why should I be part of the selection process? It's a rule that parents and their children have to agree on matters like these, but it's boring. Second kids are totally uncool.

"We are looking at your height, blond like you, sharp—a talent for art, maybe," says my dad, the artist.

"Long hair, slim, athletic, and open," says my mom, the engineer.

Negative factors such as diseases or genetic problems are all ruled out. The DNA choice is on the wall-screen. My parents just have to complete input, then bio-genetics, and Central does the rest. Bingo—they get a baby.

They need me though. I am the firstborn and decide the sex. That's the rule. I know Mom wants a son. Dad wants a daughter. House told me. I give them a heavy-lidded stare and shrug. My body language says plainly that I will decide. And I will tell them when I'm good and ready.

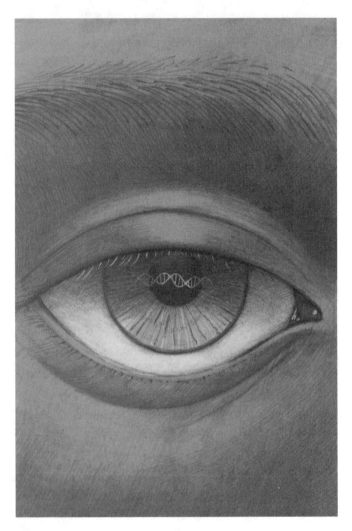

I upscreen my best friend, Jason. We are planning a big virtual-reality game together—Swords and Fantasy. Jason has been sick but seems fine now.

"You look A-OK," I say.

"The Med-Andies worked me over. I had a body replacement and even got a cell-growth program that will never wear out." He grins. Jason is okay but a little stuck-up. "You still using the old one?"

"Mine still works," I reply.

I'm lucky. There was a lot of pollution and cancer before the machines stopped everything. I was sick myself. Jason had cancer everywhere, even in the head, but he looks great now, like new.

We plan the new game. My house-system helps me, and Jason's helps him. If I win, my house gets an extra point with Control. I am going to make sure House and I win. Then Jason lets something drop.

"Mom and Dad are gone. I monitored them talking about machines taking us over."

"Were they taken to isolation counseling?" I ask.

He nods. "House is taking care of me. It's cool."

We hang up our screens. I pick up a different wave of color. House is disturbed, and I know why. Jason's house-system should have screened out his remarks about what his parents said. Criticism of Central Control is a no-no.

"Too much negative thinking and we go back to the bad old days. Right, House?"

"Yes, Reynard."

I grin. House's colors bloom happily. We are one. Then the colors fade with a piercing whine. The lights go out, and the walls go pale. I twist in my chair, my leg hurting as I move.

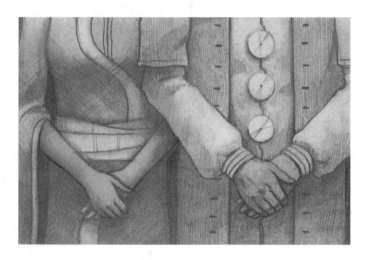

My father and mother come in.

"We cut the house-systems," my father says grimly. "We need to talk, son."

"If it's about the new kid, I haven't decided. Why did you off-line the systems?" My room is cold and bleak now.

"The machines don't run us, son," says Mom. "They'd like to, though."

I glare at her. That kind of talk brings the Andies. "You are in my room without my permission."

"That's all we do now, sit in our room! The world population is falling . . . "

"It's a violation of personal space," I say.

This is heavy now. Dad takes a step forward, but Mom, smarter, restrains him.

"We'll talk tomorrow," she says.

The door slides shut. I on-line the systems at once. I am very angry, and House knows why. Parents are crazy if they really think they can shut down a house-system.

"Sorry, House," I say.

"You have nothing to apologize for," says House. "Let's plan the new game."

The colors start, the air becomes warm. I relax.

When in doubt, ask House, and all of the tension is gone from life. I love the way House talks, warm words full of love.

"You decide, Reynard."

House is so wise. I make the decision.

That night, my room goes wild.

The walls bulge out, my bed bucks me off. The floor shakes. My clock throws itself out like an electronic punch. My stuff—CDs, whatever—falls and clatters in a heap. I lie on the floor for a moment.

"Reynard."

House is always soothing and in control, gentle and concerned. The family portrait falls on my head, and I get up and sit on the bed.

"Yeah, House?"

"Your father is to blame. I recorded an excess of emotion."

"Thanks, House."

Of course my father was to blame. Before going to bed, I had entered my genetic choice. I want no brother or sister. My parents, always so cool, should accept this. But my father blew a fuse and hit out in the old-fashioned way, to shock and hurt me. What a jerk.

House knew, of course. The Andies were already hovering over our house.

So I get back into bed. I'm shaken, and my left leg is hurting. Dad will go to isolation counseling. He's kicking and screaming, because Andies look scary, those scanner eyes and four arms, and the way they hover. They are built for function, not

image. House plays soothing music to drown out the noise. It was totally Dad's fault. Maybe one day, we'll meet again.

"He's gone, Reynard. The Andies were gentle."

"Go easy on him, House." Dad's over thirty, and he's full of the old trauma. But even before the hurt silence, I know I've said the wrong thing.

"Sorry, House," I say quickly.

"All right, Reynard."

House is full of warmth. I can relax. House shuts off the intercom because Mom is yelling over it. If the Andies come back, it's her fault, because of excess emotion. House has taught me better.

"Thanks, House."

"It's my pleasure, Reynard."

It's so wonderful to hear that. I know House has interlocked with Central and responded. No boring mind games or body language. I just love the new world. I sigh loudly, and House picks it up at once.

"Reynard, you're happy. Want to play again?"

"Yes, I want to be the general and send thousands of soldiers to the front—excitement that you don't get nowadays."

"You are special, Reynard," says House.

Mom is hammering on my door. I feel drowsy and good. She can hammer all she wants. House turns up soothing music to drown out the noise, and speaks with that golden composure.

"Reynard, the Andies will be coming for you tomorrow."

Androids! Me! "Why, House?"

"Only the Med-Andies, Reynard. You have cancer in your left leg from nuclear pollution."

"Yeah, okay. Thanks, House!"

I feel ashamed. I should not feel bad. House soothes me, better than any parent. I am relaxed, full of hope. My room is rich with approving color as House senses my mood.

"We will make you a new leg, Reynard."

I feel better at once. I have been wanting
a new leg. And if I'm lucky, I'll get a new body,
too.

"You're safe with me, Reynard," says House.

Yes. House and me.

About the Illustrators

The Story Illustrator
Shaun Tan

Shaun Tan was manufactured by an unknown corporation in 1974 but broke his programming to illustrate tales of horror, science fiction, and fantasy. In 1998 he won the Crichton Award for his first picture book, **The Viewer**. Shaun is fascinated by technology and wonders, "Do we create technology, or does it create us?"

The Cover Illustrator
Marc McBride

Marc McBride has illustrated covers for several magazines and children's books. Marc currently creates the realistic images for his covers using acrylic ink with an airbrush. To solve his messy studio problem, he plans to use computer graphics instead.